SOCIAL MEDIA
12 THINGS YOU NEED TO KNOW

by Kristin Marciniak

12 STORY LIBRARY

www.12StoryLibrary.com

12-Story Library is an imprint of Peterson Publishing Company and Press Room Editions.

Produced for 12-Story Library by Red Line Editorial

Photographs ©: william87/iStockphoto, cover, 1, 22; Antonio Guillem/iStockphoto, 4, 29; dolphfyn/Shutterstock Images, 5; Goodluz/Shutterstock Images, 6; Andresr/ Shutterstock Images, 7; Bloomua/Shutterstock Images, 8, 25; Susan Chiang/iStockphoto, 9; gradyreese/iStockphoto, 10, 28; m.jm/Shutterstock Images, 11; Jupiterimages/Creatas/ Thinkstock, 12; DragonImages/iStockphoto, 13; Monkey Business Images/Shutterstock Images, 14; Yeamake/Shutterstock Images, 15; Justin Horrocks/iStockphoto, 16; Syda Productions/Shutterstock Images, 17; SpeedKingz/Shutterstock Images, 18; omgimages/ iStockphoto, 19; Monkey Business Images/iStockphoto, 20; Monkey Business Images/ iStockphoto/Thinkstock, 21; Greg Lehman/Walla Walla Union-Bulletin/AP Images, 23; Jacek Chabraszewski/Shutterstock Images, 24; Zurijeta/Shutterstock Images, 27

ISBN
978-1-63235-223-1 (hardcover)
978-1-63235-249-1 (paperback)
978-1-62143-274-6 (hosted ebook)

Library of Congress Control Number: 2015934328

Printed in the United States of America
Mankato, MN
October, 2015

Go beyond the book. Get free, up-to-date content on this topic at 12StoryLibrary.com.

TABLE OF CONTENTS

WHAT IS SOCIAL MEDIA?

Before the Internet, most communication was a one-way street. Newspapers, magazines, radio, and TV presented the news and other information. But readers, listeners, and viewers could not participate in the conversation. Today, the Internet has made that possible. It gives the audience a chance to talk back. Social media is one way people communicate online.

Social media websites and apps allow users to post and share information. Social media users can access social media on computers, cell phones, and tablets. They share favorite videos or comment on news articles. This information, unlike an e-mail message, is public. It can be seen by many others, including family, friends, and sometimes strangers. You may never know who has seen your social media posts. You may see posts on social media without others knowing you have, too.

Many people may read your social media posts.

Social networks are a form of social media. Facebook, Twitter, and Instagram are social networks. These sites are like giant cities. Your family and friends are your neighborhood. You can connect with them to communicate and share photos and interesting links. Social networking helps you keep in touch with your digital neighbors.

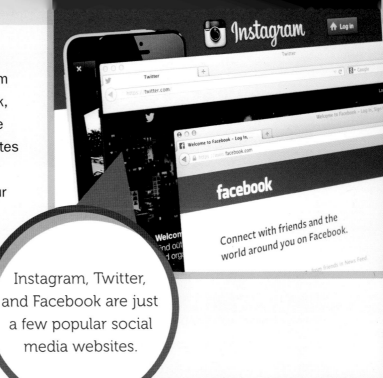

Instagram, Twitter, and Facebook are just a few popular social media websites.

Connect with friends and the world around you on Facebook.

67
Percent of Americans ages 12 and up who used social media in 2014.

- Social media is a participatory form of online communication that is public.
- Most social media use occurs on the Internet.
- Examples of social media include chatting with friends online and commenting on a news article.

2,500 YEARS OF SOCIAL MEDIA

Social media did not start on the Internet. It was "invented" in 550 BCE. That is when the first postal system was formed. Handwritten letters were delivered from one person to another. Today's social media is a lot faster. But the concept is still the same: people exchanging information and ideas across great distances.

2
WHAT CAN I DO ON SOCIAL MEDIA?

Social media helps you communicate. It can also be entertaining. Use social networks to send messages to friends. Challenge a neighbor to a game of checkers. Share photos of your latest art project. Make short videos and post them for relatives. You can even use social networks to collaborate on class projects.

Sharing things on social media is easy. Finding the right social media site can be more difficult. The most well-known sites, such as Facebook, Twitter, and Instagram, are for teenagers and adults. Kids younger than 13 are not allowed to join.

But there are sites just for kids. Create your own virtual world at Club Penguin. Connect with friends and

You can work on class projects over social media.

Kids younger than 13 can join sites such as Jabbersmack and iTwixie.

family on GeckoLife or Jabbersmack. Share your photos on Kuddle. Meet kids with similar interests on Yoursphere, Kidzworld, and iTwixie.

All of these sites provide good introductions to using social media. They are designed with your privacy and safety in mind. They are also designed for fun.

59

Percent of children who have used a social network by the age of 10.

- Social media is for entertainment and communication.
- On social media sites, you can play games, share photos, upload videos, and talk to friends and family.
- Some social media sites are designed just for kids.

IS SOCIAL MEDIA FREE?

Most social networks are free to use. There is no sign-up fee for sites such as Twitter, Facebook, and Instagram. You can make comments, post photos, and update your status information for free.

Some games, such as *Minecraft,* can be played for free.

Games are different. In many cases, you can start playing a game for free. But as you progress, you can buy extra features, such as more lives or energy. These things are not necessary to win, but they can help.

Fees for additional items are common in massively multiplayer online role-playing games (MMORPGs). These games are like virtual worlds. You create a character to represent yourself. Then you use your character to interact with other people. Some MMORPGs offer products that cost real money, such as special clothes for your character. You might also have to pay for access to members-only levels.

Some games for kids, such as *Club Penguin* and *Wizard101,* make it easy to get bonus features by

Don't use an adult's credit card without asking.

offering memberships. You pay a monthly fee for complete access to everything the site offers. Remember that you need an adult's permission before buying anything online. Keep track of exactly how much you spend. Small fees can really add up.

$4.9 billion

Estimated value of virtual items purchased in 2013.

- Most social networks are free.
- Some games are free to play but offer upgrades for a price.
- MMORPGs sometimes offer membership packages that include all of the game's extra products.

THINK ABOUT IT

Why do you think MMORPGs charge money for some services and not for others? Do you think games should charge for content? Why or why not?

IS SOCIAL MEDIA SAFE?

It is hard to know whom you can trust on the Internet. People are not always honest about who they are. You can be safe by limiting your online friends to people you actually know in real life.

Remember, everything you post on social media is public. Friends, family, and even strangers may see it. Some of your information should always remain private. Keep your real name, address, birth date, and phone number private. Do not mention the name of your school. The same goes for your financial information and Social Security number. This information is useful to people who want to find you or pretend to be you. Instead, post about activities you enjoy or your favorite sports team or band. This way, you can share your interests while keeping your private information safe.

Keep your friends list limited to people you know in real life.

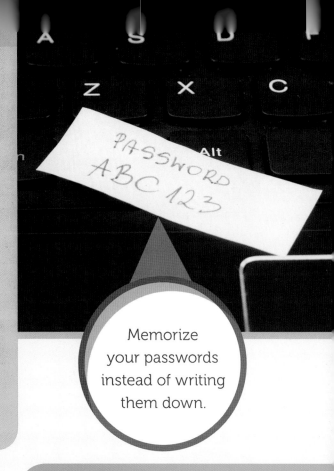

82 million

Estimated number of fake Facebook accounts.

- Limit your online friends to people you know in real life.
- Never share your name, address, birth date, phone number, school, financial information, or Social Security number.
- Only you and your parents should know your passwords.

Memorize your passwords instead of writing them down.

Closely guard your passwords. Only you and your parents should know the login information for your social media accounts. This prevents other people from accessing your private information. It also stops them from pretending to be you online. Staying safe on social media is all about smart decisions. If information is personal, keep it private.

TAG, YOU'RE HERE!

Even if you do not tell people your location, your social network might. This is called geo-tagging. It is when a social network includes your location on a post. It is especially common when you use cell phones or tablets. You can tell your social networks to stop geo-tagging. Ask an adult how to disable it on your accounts and devices.

11

SHOULD I SHARE MY ACCOUNTS WITH MY PARENTS?

Learning how to use social media safely is like learning to tie your shoes or ride a bike. It takes a lot of practice. This is true even for social media sites made just for kids. Most will not let you sign up without help from a parent or guardian. Those sites also give your guardian access to your account.

Sharing your social media passwords with your parents helps you stay safe. It is not an invasion of your privacy. The Children's Online Privacy Protection Act (COPPA) says websites may not collect information from people younger than 13. Younger kids are especially vulnerable to marketing companies. They might unknowingly share too much information with websites.

Share your passwords with a trusted adult.

Sharing images and posts on social media can include the whole family.

COPPA says companies may not collect the names and e-mail addresses of kids younger than 13. That information is usually required to join a social media site. That is why kids' social networks require parental approval. It is also why most social media sites do not allow users younger than 13.

If you are not 13 years old yet, ask your parents or guardians to help you sign up on a kids-only social media site. Or ask them to share their social media sites with you. Ask to see family photos on Instagram. Sit down with them when they browse their social networks. Ask questions. Together, you can learn about social media. You can decide what rules work for your family.

61
Percent of parents who monitor their children's social networking activity.

- Most kids' social media sites require permission from a parent or guardian.
- COPPA prevents websites from collecting information about people younger than 13.
- Ask an adult for help signing up for a kids-only social network if you are younger than 13.

WHAT SHOULDN'T I POST ON SOCIAL MEDIA?

Posting a message on social media is not the same as writing in your journal. Other people can see everything you write or share. Unlike something written on a piece of paper, things posted on the Internet might stay there forever. Even if you delete a post or an e-mail, a backup might exist. Some people might even have saved the message to their own computers. Your name will be linked to it forever.

It is easy to be brave behind a computer screen. People are more likely to say mean things online than they are in real life. But if you post hurtful things, you do more than hurt someone else's feelings. You also make yourself look bad. Information you share on social media never really goes away. Future friends, colleges, and even bosses may find it years later. That is why it is smart to avoid

Writing your thoughts in a journal keeps them private.

A HISTORY IN TWEETS

All American tweets, or posts, made on Twitter are archived at the Library of Congress. It is part of the library's effort to "collect the story of America." And it is a big job. More than 400 million tweets are sent by Americans every day. As of early 2013, there were more than 170 billion tweets on file.

sharing gossip and put-downs on social media. The same goes for using offensive language or sharing private information. Before you post anything online, ask yourself, "Would I want my grandma to see this?" If the answer is no, then do not post it.

49
Percent of people ages 10 to 18 who have posted something on social media they later regretted.

- Assume everything you post on the Internet stays online forever, even if you delete it.
- Do not post gossip, offensive language, or private information.
- Ask yourself, "Would I want my grandma to see this?"

Your tweets are stored in the Library of Congress.

See what's happening in your world.

Twitter
Twitter, Inc.

WHAT SHOULD I POST ON SOCIAL MEDIA?

Sharing something on social media is like shouting it through a megaphone. That is why many people create a persona when they use social media. They are selective about the information they share or post. They know many people, even strangers, will be able to see, read, and share it. Often, these personas include only positive things. Most people are not eager to share bad news or unflattering photos.

To create a positive online persona, make sure your posts show you at

> Keep the things you share on social media positive.

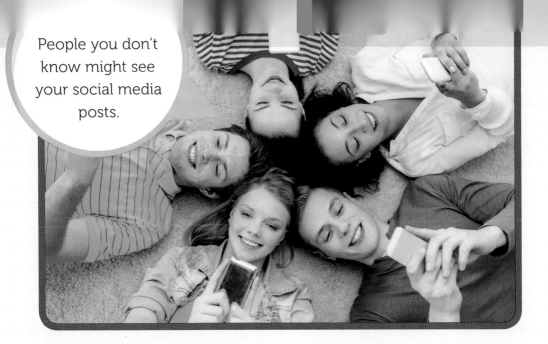

People you don't know might see your social media posts.

your best. Share accomplishments you are proud of, such as performing in a piano recital. When you comment on someone else's posts, keep your words and tone positive.

You can use social media to thank or recognize someone else. Positive messages on social media are powerful. It feels good to make someone smile. Positivity can be contagious, too. Others will share your nice comments and be inspired to post some of their own.

Social media is not limited to words. You can also share pictures. Post photos of your latest artistic creation or a family celebration. Before posting, make sure everyone in the picture is okay with your posting it.

Some people are uncomfortable having their faces or names on the Internet.

45 million
Number of pictures posted on Instagram every day.

- Use social media to share accomplishments that make you proud.
- Compliment a friend or family member on social media.
- Ask people before posting photographs of them.

17

WHAT IF SOMEONE BOTHERS ME ON SOCIAL MEDIA?

Some people do not follow the rules of social media. They use social media to share embarrassing, untrue, or negative information about other people. Cyberbullies often use social media to bully others.

But there are ways to combat a bully like this. First, do not respond to any messages from bullies. Instead, record the times and dates of when you were bullied. Print out a copy or take a picture of the message. That is your evidence the bullying occurred.

Cyberbullying happens online, often on social media sites.

Imagine that your friend is being cyberbullied. What advice would you give him or her?

You can report the bully to the social media site. Even if the bully hides behind a fake name, the company might be able to learn his or her real identity. They might ban the bully from using the site. If the bully is from your school, report him or her to the principal. Sometimes, bullying messages you receive are threatening or make you uncomfortable. If this is the case, ask for an adult's help immediately and report the bully to the police.

Cyberbullying is against the law in all 50 states. Make sure your social media experience stays positive. Always tell an adult if someone is bullying you or making you feel uncomfortable.

50

Number of states with laws that address cyberbullying.

- Cyberbullies are people who use social media to share embarrassing, untrue, or negative information about others.
- Do not respond to bullies, but save the messages and tell an adult.
- Depending on the situation, you should also report the bully to the social media site where you were harassed, to the police, and to your school.

Cyberbullying can affect life at school, too.

19

CAN SOCIAL MEDIA HELP ME LEARN?

Social media has changed the way people communicate. You can post your thoughts as soon as you have them. Social media allows you to share information and ideas 24 hours a day.

These changes in communication also affect schools. Social media has changed the way students collaborate, or work together. You can plan a project and exchange ideas in private chat rooms or on bulletin boards. Share interesting articles and pictures. Connect with classmates by video chat. Some teachers list assignments on a classroom blog and encourage

Does your teacher use social media in the classroom?

You might use social media to help with homework.

students to comment. One teacher in Brooklyn, New York, uses Twitter to share resources and tips for studying. Schools can send tweets or texts about upcoming events.

Some social media sites are just for schools. Sites like Edmodo and Schoology let teachers set up virtual classrooms. Students take quizzes and submit assignments online. Teachers give feedback on student work. Discussions started during the school day can be continued after the final bell rings. You can check your school's social media pages for updates on events. Thanks to social media, the classroom never closes.

59

Percent of schools with students who use social media for educational purposes.

- Social media has changed the way people communicate.
- Students use social media to work on group projects and share interesting information.
- Social media sites designed just for schools allow teachers and students to communicate after the school day is over.

HOW CAN I USE SOCIAL MEDIA TO CONNECT?

Social media can connect you with people across the globe. But it is also great for making connections at home. With just a few clicks of your keypad, you can find neighbors who share your interests. Join a skateboarding club. Exchange favorite books. Big cities seem like close-knit communities when you make friends on social media.

THINK ABOUT IT

Some people say social media actually makes people less social. Do you agree or disagree? Why? List at least three reasons.

You can connect with all sorts of people over social media.

54.2

Percent of people ages 13 to 24 who volunteered in their communities in 2011.

- Social media makes it easy to find people with similar interests.
- Several apps offer suggestions for local volunteering opportunities.
- Spread the word about a charity of your choice on social media.

Social media helped the ALS Ice Bucket Challenge go viral.

Social media is also helpful for those who want to get more involved in their community. Many charities and community organizations can be found on social media. They use social networks to build relationships with volunteers and donors.

Social media is a great tool to spread the word about a cause close to your heart. You can post about why a cause is important to you. You can even ask your family and friends to volunteer with you.

ALS ICE BUCKET CHALLENGE

In August 2014, the ALS Association issued a challenge over social media. The charity raises money for research on ALS, a serious illness. It encouraged its followers to ask their friends to donate to the ALS Association and dump a bucket of ice water over their heads. The challenge went viral and raised more than $220 million. Even President Obama participated.

DO SOCIAL NETWORKS BENEFIT FROM HAVING ME AS A USER?

Social networks are businesses. They exist to make money. They do this by selling advertisements. The price of an ad is based on how many people view it. More users means the sites make more money.

> Online ads try to convince you to purchase something.

You might have a lot of fun using social media. But to social networks, you are a commodity. Social networks know a lot about their users: age, gender, location, and even personal interests. This information is used to create advertisements for specific users. People who list cooking as one of their hobbies might see advertisements from local grocery stores on their social media news feeds. They might see ads for the latest kitchen gadget.

Many companies have their own social media pages. They use them to communicate with customers. Often, they share special offers or

You might see an ad on social media for an online game. deals with the hope that you will buy their product or service. In 2011, the New York Jets used their Twitter account to give away tickets. They wanted the contest to increase fan loyalty. The Jets hoped these fans would spend more money in the future.

$14 billion

Estimated annual spending on social media advertising by companies by 2018.

- Social networks make money by selling advertisements.
- The more people who use a social network, the more money the social network can make.
- Social networks track information and behavior to target advertisements to specific users.

12

DO I NEED TO BE ON SOCIAL MEDIA?

Social media is a good way to communicate and make friends. But nobody needs to be on social media. It is not a basic need, such as food, water, or shelter. You do not need it to be successful in school. And there are plenty of other ways to keep in touch with family and friends. Just let people know how they can reach you. Let them know if they should use the phone, send an e-mail, or visit you in person.

People spend hours a day on social media. This is often more than they spend socializing in real life. Social media seems to be all about connecting with others. But some research suggests that when you are on social media too much, it has a negative effect. In 2012, a study found that using Facebook could increase anxiety and feelings that you are not good enough.

If you choose to take part in social media, set limits for yourself. Check your account just once or twice a day. Do not compare yourself to the things you see on social media. Remember, most people use social media to show themselves at their best. Their posts and shares have

28
Percent of the world's population who are active users of social media.

- You do not need to use social media to be successful in school or to keep in touch with your family and friends.
- If you do use social media, limit the amount of time you spend on it.
- Social media is a form of entertainment. If you are not having fun anymore, do not use it.

created positive personas. Their lives might look perfect on social media. But they have problems and worries just like you. Social media is like any other hobby: Use it if you enjoy it. If it stops being fun, do something else.

Remember to get out and have fun with friends in real life.

FACT SHEET

- The first social networking site appeared in 1997. It was called Six Degrees. Like today's Facebook, Six Degrees connected people who knew each other or who had similar interests. But only 22.1 percent of Americans used the Internet in 1997. Six Degrees had only 3 million users. Today, Facebook has 1.44 billion active monthly users. With so few users, a person's social network on Six Degrees was pretty small. The site closed in 2001.

- Social media is not always used for entertainment. Eighty percent of law enforcement officials use social media to gather information during investigations. In most cases, law enforcement agencies have to follow the same rules as everyone else. They cannot demand to see someone's private posts unless there is an immediate threat to public safety. But many people do not have any privacy settings on their accounts. If officers can see someone's social media profile, it can be used to build a case against a suspect.

- Social media is a global medium, but it cannot be accessed everywhere. China, Iran, and North Korea have blocked Facebook, Twitter, and YouTube. YouTube also is not allowed in Pakistan or Eritrea, a country in Africa. Facebook cannot be accessed in Vietnam. In most cases, the bans exist to prevent people from posting anti-government content. Other countries, such as Bangladesh, Afghanistan, and Syria, have banned the use of social media during short periods of political unrest.

- Social media can play a big part in social and political change. This was evident during the Arab Spring in 2011, when people in North Africa and the Middle East protested their governments. People in those regions shared their feelings on Facebook and Twitter. These conversations led to major events, such as public rallies and the resignations of world leaders. The entire world witnessed these events on YouTube and online news sites, which spread the revolution even further.

GLOSSARY

audience
The people who watch, read, or listen to something.

commodity
A product that is bought and sold.

geo-tagging
The process of adding location information to a post on social media.

media
The methods through which information is communicated to the public.

network
A group of people or groups who are connected to one another by a common interest.

persona
A partial identity you create to represent yourself in a specific situation.

social media
Any website that allows interaction between users.

status
Something going on in your life that you share on social media.

tweet
A post on Twitter, a social media website.

virtual
Existing on computers or on the Internet.

FOR MORE INFORMATION

Books

Burgan, Michael, and Angie Kaelberer. *The Making of the Social Network: An Interactive Modern History Adventure.* Mankato, MN: Capstone, 2014.

McHugh, Jeff. *Maintaining a Positive Digital Footprint.* Ann Arbor, MI: Cherry Lake, 2014.

Rowell, Rebecca. *Social Media: Like It or Leave It.* North Mankato, MN: Compass Point, 2015.

Small, Cathleen. *Make the Most of Facebook and Other Social Media.* New York: Cavendish Square, 2015.

Websites

Best Apps for Kids
www.bestappsforkids.com

New York Public Library: Internet Safety Tips for Children and Teens
www.nypl.org/help/about-nypl/legal-notices/internet-safety-tips

SafeKids.com: Kids' Rules for Online Safety
www.safekids.com/kids-rules-for-online-safety

INDEX

About the Author

Kristin Marciniak writes the books she wishes she had read when she was in school. She's written about the Navy SEALs, the United States Coast Guard, the Salem Witch Trials, and other wild times in American history.

READ MORE FROM 12-STORY LIBRARY

Every 12-Story Library book is available in many formats, including Amazon Kindle and Apple iBooks. For more information, visit your device's store or 12StoryLibrary.com.